T0195686

I LOVE
L(the)ORD

Suzanne Pavlick

WESTBOW
PRESS®
A DIVISION OF THOMAS NELSON
& ZONDERVAN

WestBow Press books may be ordered through booksellers or by contacting:

WestBow Press
A Division of Thomas Nelson & Zondervan
1663 Liberty Drive
Bloomington, IN 47403
www.westbowpress.com
1 (866) 928-1240

ISBN: 978-1-5127-3037-1 (sc)
ISBN: 978-1-5127-3038-8 (e)

Library of Congress Control Number: 2016902049

Print information available on the last page.

WestBow Press rev. date: 3/10/2016

This book is dedicated to the most magnificent of all, the Lord Jesus Christ.

My children Marylou (Sunflower) and John Pavlick (Superhero) my two precious treasures. They have been so supportive and positive, they kept me going and said never give up do what makes you happy. I thank them for putting up with me and for all the help they have given me. Thank you for all your patience. Thank you for loving me, supporting me and being there for me.

I love them more than words can say. I don't know where I'd be without them they are my everything. There aren't enough words to tell you how much I love you.

ACKNOWLEDGMENTS

Marlene Hershey (Author & Musician)- Thank you for your guidance, support, encouragement and all your love. I don't know where I would be without you! My dear friend you are such a wonderful, kind & caring person. Thank you for your daily encouragement!

Susan Waters (Author, Speaker & performance coach)- Thank you for all your help, support and love. Thanks for pushing me when I needed it. I'm so thankful & grateful to have a friend like you!!! "You are not only amazing you are true through and through I am so happy God led me to you my dear friend. You are the most supportive person I know. You're always so Positive, Uplifting, Honest, Kind, Generous, Caring and so Empowering and it really shows. I'm so Thankful & Grateful for your Amazing Beautiful Friendship! I'm so happy we both made a decision to be dear friends. You are a Beautiful Treasure & I do Treasure you."

I would like to extend a heartfelt Thank you to my parents for always being there. Thank you for all your support, guidance, direction and love. Thank you for being such amazing parents!! I am truly blessed.

I would like to thank my publisher West Bow Press and all the staff who helped my book to fruition.

Be all you can be by opening up your heart and mind and showing compassion toward others and letting them know you care. Be kind to everyone, say nice things to all people. Your words can change someone's day. Reach out to others. Be the kind of person you want your children to see. You are their Greatest influence. Be the compassionate, kind, courteous, caring, loving person for the world to see. You can make such a huge difference. **BE THE LIGHT FOR ALL TO SEE BE THE WAY GOD WANTS YOU TO BE. S.P.**

Compassionate people have the most beautiful hearts. They have experienced suffering, defeat, struggles and loss. They know deep down how to be sensitive and gentle toward others. That is what fills their hearts with such warmth and love. Compassionate, caring, warm loving people don't just happen, it comes from within their beautiful hearts. Suzanne Pavlick

DON'T

DON'T BE JEALOUS OF ONE ANOTHER, BE HAPPY FOR ONE ANOTHER.

DON'T KNOCK EACH OTHER DOWN, BUILD EACH OTHER UP.

DON'T HATE ONE ANOTHER, INSTEAD LOVE ONE ANOTHER.

DON'T JUDGE ONE ANOTHER, COMPLIMENT ONE ANOTHER.

DON'T SPEAK TO OTHERS WITH HARSH, NASTY, HURTFUL AND HATEFUL WORDS. SPEAK TO OTHERS WITH KIND, CARING, LOVING WORDS.

DON'T TREAT OTHERS WITH DISRESPECT AND HATE, INSTEAD TREAT OTHERS WITH RESPECT AND LOVE.

DON'T TURN YOUR BACK ON THOSE REACHING OUT TO YOU, INSTEAD OPEN YOUR HEART AND YOUR MIND. REACH OUT TO THEM, YOU CAN MAKE A DIFFERENCE.

Suzanne Pavlick 8/26/2015

"Don't should've, could've or would've on yourself or anyone else. Can you hear yourself saying, I should have done it that way or I could have done it this way but what IF I would have done it the other way??? COULD'VE, SHOULD'VE, WOULD'VE, we all do it with so many things in life. We are putting stress and pressure on ourselves instead of BELIEVING in ourselves. STOP SHOULDing, COULDing & WOULDing ON YOURSELVES! Instead say I will, I can, It will work out. Be positive and Believe in yourselves. God believes in you."

DON'T EVER LET ANYONE
MAKE YOU FEEL HATED,
UNLOVED, UNWANTED,
NOT GOOD ENOUGH,
USELESS, HOPELESS,
UNWORTHY & ALONE.
IT'S NOT ABOUT YOU,
IT'S ABOUT THEM.
BE AROUND THOSE
THAT ARE TRULY
POSITIVE, SUPPORTIVE,
ENCOURAGING &
LOVING!! YOU DESERVE
IT!!! YOUR WORTH IT!!!
SUZANNE PAVLICK

ELEVATE ENCOURAGE EMPOWER EXPRESS ENGAGE

Engage with others in a positive way. Encourage others to do their best, let them know you believe in them and support them. Elevate all those around you with their goals and dreams even when they think they can't do it. Don't let them give up encourage them to go forward. Express to them that they can do it don't let anyone or anything stop them! Empower them with Positive words, actions. You can be someone's greatest impact in life! Let them know how Excellent, Exceptional and Extraordinary they are! This is an Excellent way to be with all people. You will get such a feeling of elation, enjoyment and excitement.

Suzanne Pavlick

We are all equal in this world no matter our skin color, background, religion, financial status, social status, etc. We are all human beings on earth. No human being was born to hate they were taught too hate. If they can be taught too hate they can be taught too love. We were all born with a Heart and what we allow in our Hearts and minds is a choice. We choose to love or hate. No one controls what is on the inside of our hearts. If we choose love, compassion and total acceptance for others, the world would be a happier, peaceful place. What's inside your heart and mind? Do you judge others? Do you have hate in your heart? Are you jealous of others? Do you despise others? Can you accept others no matter what? Can you accept them for their flaws? Can you accept them even if their poor, ill, disabled, so on and so forth? Can you accept All no matter what? Can you accept ALL no matter what walk of life anyone comes from? Do you love and accept ALL people the way the Lord loves and accepts ALL? We all want to make a place in the world and we all can with Love. Love ALL unconditionally no matter what. Open your hearts and minds to God. GOD'S WAY IS THE MOST BEAUTIFUL, PEACEFUL PATHWAY OF LIFE. With God in your heart you can also love ALL unconditionally, accept All no matter what. Open your hearts, love one another, respect each other, reach out to each other, help each other, encourage and support each other, forgive each other, be kind to each other, etc. In this life we are all on a journey that's what makes us different. None of our journeys are the same, but it doesn't make you better or less than anyone. WE ARE ALL EQUAL! Let your life have purpose on purpose, let your life speak loud with love, let it be a message for all to hear and see the way God wants you to be.

PRAY FOR EACH OTHER.

LOVE EVERYONE UNCONDITIONALLY NO MATTER WHAT THE SAME WAY THE LORD LOVES YOU.

Suzanne Pavlick

FATHER, FAMILY, AND FRIENDS

Our true fortunes are right in front of us and for a lot of us we don't see it. We are too busy worrying about everything else that we can't see what is right in front of us. We get caught up in everyday life with our jobs, children, running from place to place, meeting deadlines, so on and so forth that the most important things and people in our lives take a back seat sort of speak. For some, fame and fortune take over and some get so lost in it, it becomes the first and foremost thing in their lives. They are so fascinated with all the attention and glamour, they can't see their true fortunes in front of them. They even forget about our FATHER, THE GREAT ALMIGHTY. You can have that fortune if you just take the time to be with the Father daily and set special time aside to be with your family and friends. That is where the real fortune lies and that is priceless! All the money, fame, glamour and attention in the world can't buy you or give you Love, Peace, Joy or Happiness. THE FATHER, FAMILY AND FRIENDS ARE ALL A PRICELESS TREASURE!!

Suzanne Pavlick

"Feed your faith instead of feeding your fears. Fear will cripple you, crumble you & make a prisoner out of you." Suzanne Pavlick

"NEVER JUDGE ONE ANOTHER, ALWAYS LOVE ONE ANOTHER."

"HOLDING ONTO REGRETS ONLY HOLDS US PRISONERS WITHIN OURSELVES."

"It's nice to be appreciated and it's nice to be appreciative."

"ONE OF THE MOST POWERFUL THINGS YOU CAN DO FOR YOURSELF IS TO FORGIVE OTHERS. IT IS THE MOST FREEING THING YOU CAN DO FOR YOURSELF. IT IS THE MOST PEACEFUL FEELING ON THE INSIDE.FORGIVE OTHERS AS GOD HAS FORGIVEN YOU. LOVE YOUR ENEMIES, PRAY FOR THOSE WHO HURT YOU, BETRAY YOU, USE YOU, ABUSE YOU, TALK ABOUT YOU, TALK DOWN TO YOU, DISRESPECT YOU & EVEN TURNED THEIR BACK ON YOU. IT'S NOT ABOUT YOU, IT ALL HAS TO DO WITH THEM. ALWAYS FORGIVE YOURSELF. LET GO AND LET GOD TAKE IT." Suzanne Pavlick

FORGIVENESS FOR ALL

FORGIVING OTHERS IS THE BEST THING YOU CAN DO FOR YOURSELF. FORGIVE OTHERS AS GOD HAS FORGIVEN YOU. LOVE AND PRAY FOR YOUR ENEMIES. PRAY FOR THOSE WHO HURT YOU, BETRAYED YOU, USE YOU, ABUSE YOU, TALK ABOUT YOU, TALK DOWN TO YOU, DISRESPECT YOU AND EVEN TURN THEIR BACK ON YOU. IT'S NOT ABOUT YOU IT ALL HAS TO DO WITH THEM. LET GO AND LET GOD TAKE IT.

YOU CAN BE FREE THROUGH THE ALMIGHTY

Some of us go through traumatic events in our lives from the time we were little all the way through adulthood. We have no self-esteem, no confidence in ourselves. Some of us are full of rage, anger, despair, depression, sadness, hopelessness, feeling unworthy, never good enough. We keep everything bottled up on the inside of us. We don't talk about it with anyone, we're afraid of what others might think of us. We are too embarrassed and ashamed and filled with so much guilt. We don't realize the ugliness it creates on the inside of us. We think we are fine, we put on that fake smile like all is perfect, when deep down inside a fire burns within us. Some use drugs and alcohol to ease the pain, others are just always angry and lash out at others and unfortunately some commit suicide. We blame ourselves for it all and it's really not our fault. All that ugliness is hiding deep in your heart and we just go through the motions of life. We pretend to be happy and full of joy, but on the inside some are going off like explosives. For some their lives have been torn apart piece by piece from the time they were little. Whatever it may be from: Physical, Sexual, Verbal. Mental Abuse, Rape, Being Bullied, ETC, YOU CAN BE FREE!!!A lot of people carry heavy burdens all their lives not realizing how sick it's making them on the inside. They are locked away behind all the ugliness and shame. Don't be afraid to let it all go!! Talk about it!! Get it out!! YOU CAN BE FREE FROM THIS PRISON!!!!!!Remember, it's not your fault, be willing to forgive so you can live. Forgiving those who hurt you, who caused you pain, abused you, made you feel less than, turned their back on you, etc, forgiving them is the most peaceful thing you can do for yourself. Some may say I don't know how to forgive and let go. Try to think of it this way, Forgiveness is a choice, you can choose to stay a prisoner to those who have hurt or wronged you and remain that way and keep giving them power over your life or you can choose to be happy and free the way God wants you to be. You can choose to stay inside that cage and be a prisoner to anger, rage, fear, resentment, hurt, pain, bitterness, regret, shame, sorrow, disappointment, blame etc. Ask yourself, do I want to be a prisoner to all this ugliness forever? Do I want to give those who hurt or wronged me the power over my life over how I feel?

You can take away all their power once you forgive them and forgive yourself. You can be set free and begin to heal. Open your heart and mind to God. God will take all your heavy burdens from you. You can talk to God day and night he is always there to listen. Believe and trust him with all your heart. God is compassionate, loving, forgiving, understanding and so gentle. You are his precious child he loves you no matter what, he is your greatest comforter. Surrender everything to the Almighty, he is your truest friend he will never turn his back on you. As you let it all go and give it all to the Almighty you will have such a great feeling a beautiful release. You will feel such freedom and peace within yourself and so much joy in your heart it's such an amazing flutter!!

YOU CAN BE FREE!!!!!!!!!!

"TODAY IS FRIDAY, A NEW DAY, ALL YOU HAVE TO DO IS WALK WITH GOD IN HIS WAY. FOLLOW HIM ALONG AND SING A NEW SONG. OPEN YOUR HEART AND LET GOD LEAD THE WAY. HE WILL NEVER LEAD YOU ASTRAY. HE WILL GUIDE YOU TO A WHOLE NEW WAY."

"IT'S SATURDAY!! HOPEFULLY THE FIRST THING YOU DID WAS PRAY! WE SHOULD PRAY EVERYDAY, SEVERAL TIMES A DAY AND PRAISE GOD! HIS MERCIES ARE NEW EVERYDAY! GOD WANTS TO HEAR FROM YOU ALWAYS. GOD WANTS TO KNOW WHAT IS ON YOUR HEART AND MIND. GIVE IT ALL TO GOD, TRUST AND BELIEVE HIM WITH ALL YOU GOT! GOD WILL TAKE THE HEAVINESS FROM YOUR HEART. HE MAKES ALL THINGS NEW!"

"GOOD SUNDAY MORNING!! I HOPE YOU ALL PRAYED AND PRAISED THE GOOD LORD THIS MORNING!! I PRAY YOU ALL HAVE A DAY OF SUNSHINE, HAPPINESS, PEACE, JOY AND LOVE. I PRAY YOU ALL HAVE A WONDERFUL DAY AND THAT WHATEVER COMES YOUR WAY YOU DEAL WITH IT IN A GODLY WAY. I PRAY YOU ALL HAVE A POSITIVE AND EMPOWERING DAY!! I PRAY YOU ALL LOVE ONE ANOTHER THE WAY THE ALMIGHTY GOD LOVES YOU!"

How fast life changes in just moments, then you see something that turns it back around, this is so Awesome!!! That is the power of Jesus!!

WHAT A BEAUTIFUL DAY THE LORD HAS MADE!! DON'T FORGET TO THANK GOD FOR WAKING YOU UP TODAY!! GOD IS A MAGNIFICENT, BEAUTIFUL GOD

GOD LOVES ALL, GOD IS AMAZING, WONDERFUL, LOVING, KIND, COMPASSIONATE & THE MOST POWERFUL OF ALL

LIVE, LAUGH, LOVE. ENJOY EVERY MOMENT OF YOUR LIFE!!

GOD IS FAITHFUL FOREVER AND EVER WITHOUT A DOUBT.

"The only opinion you should worry about is god's opinion and he loves you more than you can imagine" Suzanne Pavlick

"I PRAY FOR EVERYONE TO BE BLESSED WITH MIRACLES FOR YOUR DREAMS TOO COME TRUE. MAY YOU ALL HAVE PEACE, LOVE AND JOY IN YOUR HEART."

"DON'T EVER WALK IN ANYONE'S SHADOW, ONLY WALK IN THE SHADOW OF THE LORD THE ONE AND ONLY TRUE LIGHT OF THE WORLD."

"TEXTING and DRIVING is just as bad as someone who is TEXTING and TALKING to you face to face, THE FOCUS ISN'T ON YOU EITHER, LIFE IS PRECIOUS!"

"HIS LOVE IS SO PURE, BREATHTAKING AND ENDLESS."

"I PRAY FOR EVERYONE TO BE THOUGHTFUL, KIND AND ENCOURAGING TO OTHERS. YOU CAN MAKE A DIFFERENCE IN SOMEONE'S LIFE."

"GOD WILL GUIDE YOU ALONG THE MOST BEAUITIFUL PATH OF LIFE, TRUST AND BELIEVE IN HIM WITH ALL YOUR HEART."

"BE GOOD TO GOD, HE IS ALWAYS GOOD TO YOU, HE KEEPS HIS PROMISES AND HIS LOVE IS ENDLESS TOO, NEVER DOUBT HIM, HE ALWAYS COMES THROUGH."

"MAGNIFICENT MASTER OF THE UNIVERSE! THE GREATEST LOVE OF ALL!"

"ACCEPTANCE IS THE KEY TO HAPPINESS, PEACE, JOY AND LOVE. IT ENABLES YOU TO ACCEPT OTHERS FOR WHO THEY ARE AND LOVE THEM UNCONDITIONALLY, LOVE THEM THE WAY JESUS LOVES YOU."

"TOMORROW STARTS A NEW BOOK IN YOUR LIFE, MAKE IT POSITIVE, EMPOWERING, INSPIRING, HAPPY, PEACEFUL, JOYFUL AND LOVING NOT ONLY FOR YOU BUT TO IMPACT THE WORLD! BE A BEAUTIFUL LIGHT FOR ALL THE WORLD TO SEE! THE WAY JESUS WANTS YOU TOO BE."

"If you know someone who is struggling, open your heart and reach out to them, even it's just to give them a hug, show them you care"

"No one ever really knows how much pain someone is really in on the inside or how dark their world really is"

"FORGIVENESS IS A DEEP PEACE WITHIN YOURSELF, A QUIET CALMNESS, THE RELEASE OF HEAVY BURDENS"

"You are the most influential person in your children's lives, spend time with them, guide them, nurture them, Love them and Pray with them."

"Your words and actions are powerful, the way you act and speak can impact others lives, Speak, Listen and Act with Love."

"Letting go of the pain of our past is one of the most Miraculous things we can do for ourselves."

"Always remember, never say good-bye always say see you soon"

"Always tell your family and friends you love them no matter what. Don't go to bed angry, no one knows what tomorrow brings. Open your heart, be forgiving. Don't live with regrets because then it's too late."

"Depression is like a lion within ROARING to get out!"

Forgiving others is the best thing you can do for yourself it's the most peaceful feeling on the inside. Forgive others as God has forgiven you. Love your enemies. Pray for those who spitefully hurt you.

"MAKE A DIFFERENCE IN SOMEONE'S LIFE. OPEN YOUR HEART. SAY SOMETHING TO IMPACT THEM AND MAKE THEIR HEART HAPPY."

GOD, THE ULTIMATE HIDING PLACE.....ALWAYS TRUST IN HIM

"You can do anything just put your mind to it! You can do it! Pray because God will carry you the rest of the way."

You can change your life by changing your attitude, opening up your heart and mind to the word of God.

What if the whole world could all just love one another, accept each other, respect one another, encourage one another, help one another, and all love, praise, and worship God? What a Beautiful Breathtaking World this would be!!

NOTHING WILL EVER PUT THAT FIRE OUT!!! HE IS A MAGNIFICENT GOD!!

"The more people have the more they want, that is Greed they are the insecure, jealous, & very unhappy people."

"I CAN ONLY IMAGINE BEING IN YOUR PRESENCE SURROUNDED BY YOUR GLORY, WALKING BESIDE YOU HAND IN HAND AS MY JOURNEY IS ABOUT TO START. I FEEL SUCH A WARM PEACEFUL FEELING COME OVER ME. I FEEL AS IF I'M FLOATING, I FEEL SO FREE. JUST KNOWING YOU ARE WITH ME JESUS AND THIS IS GOING TO BE THE BEAUTIFUL PLACE I WILL BE FOR ETERNITY." Suzanne Pavlick

THINK ABOUT HOW YOU REALLY TREAT OTHERS BY YOUR ACTIONS, INACTIONS, YOUR WORDS, YOUR SILENCE. DO YOU SPITEFULLY IGNORE OTHERS, JUDGE OTHERS, PUSH THEM AWAY, MAKE THEM FEEL LIKETHEY NO LONGER EXIST? YOU CAN HAVE A HUGE IMPACT ON SOMEONE. YOU CAN EITHER LIFT THEM UP, ENCOURAGE THEM, MAKE THEM LAUGH, MAKE THEM FEEL LIKE THEY ARE SOMEONE OR TEAR THEM DOWN AND RIP THEIR HEART OUT, LEAVING THEM TO FEEL UNWORTHY, USELESS, HOPELESS, UNWANTED & ALONE. THINK ABOUT HOW YOU WANT TO BE TREATED. THINK HOW IT WOULD MAKE YOU FEEL. REMEMBER DEATH AND LIFE ARE IN THE POWER OF THE TONGUE. SUZANNE PAVLICK

"Some of us say IF I could of? IF they don't like it? IF I'm not good enough? IF I'm too old or young? What IF it doesn't work out? We IF ourselves about everything and we create doubt in ourselves. We stop ourselves from going forward in life because we IF ourselves way too much. Don't IF yourself! When you IF yourself you're putting doubt in yourselves. Take IF out of your vocabulary and say yes it will. Believe in yourselves. And remember with God all things are possible." Suzanne Pavlick

"THE OPEN DOOR OF FAITH

So many doors in our lives have been closed, opportunities lost. There is always a reason for something like this. You have to have Faith and believe in God with all your heart, mind and soul. The doors have been shut for a reason. God wants to take you to a new plateau. God has Treasures for you beyond your wildest dreams. Keep praying and believing with all your heart because the Father can open doors no man can shut. There is a secret key to your dreams it is The Father, The Almighty, THE GREATEST!!!!!"

"NEVER LET ANYONE OR ANYTHING STEAL YOUR JOY, HAPPINESS, PEACE OR LOVE. HOLD ONTO THESE IN YOUR HEART. NEVER LET ANYTHING NEGATIVE CONTROL YOU, NEGATIVITY CREATES FEELINGS OF HATE, ANGER, ETC. NEVER GIVE AWAY YOUR POWER TO ANYONE!! NOTHING AND NO ONE IN THIS WORLD IS WORTH LOSING IT TO!! HAVING JOY, PEACE, HAPPINESS & LOVE IN YOUR HEART IS WORTH MORE THAN ALL THE MONEY IN THE WORLD!! YOU ARE TO VALUABLE & PRECIOUS!!" GOD LOVES YOU!! SUZANNE PAVLICK 11 /2014

YOUR LOVE

YOUR LOVE I FEEL FROM MILLIONS OF MILES AWAY. I RECEIVE YOUR GIFTS FROM AFAR. I FEEL YOU ALWAYS AROUND ME. I TURN TO YOU AND YOUR ALWAYS THERE WITH YOUR ARMS OUTSTRETCHED TO HOLD ME AND SHOW ME YOU CARE AND TO TELL ME YOU'LL ALWAYS BE THERE. YOUR LOVE IS DEEPER THAN THE DEEPEST BLUE SEA, OH HOW I LOVE MY FATHER THE GREAT ALMIGHTY!

I'm deeply saddened to see and hear all the hate going on in this world. What happened to respect, love, kindness, appreciation, treating others with dignity and grace? Is the way you treat others the same way you treat your own family? Think about how you treat others. Do you treat them the way you want to be treated? Why is it so hard for everyone to open their hearts and minds to being loving, kind & helpful to all no matter where they come from or who they are? We are all equal in this world. No one is better than anyone else. Can you imagine if we all loved one another, respected each other, helped one another? Ask yourself how you would want others to treat you or someone in your family? Life is too short to be hateful, angry, rageful, jealous, etc. Open your hearts and treat others with love, kindness & respect. Reach out and help others in need. It takes more energy to hate than it does to love.

Suzanne Pavlick 11/20/2015

"SOME PEOPLE WONDER WHY OTHERS FEEL WORTHLESS, DEPRESSED, LONELY & HURT. ESPECIALLY WHEN THEY HAVE BEEN NOTHING BUT NICE. THINK ABOUT HOW YOU MAKE PEOPLE FEEL. DO YOU TURN YOUR BACK ON THEM AND THROW THEM AWAY LIKE YESTERDAY'S TRASH? YOUR ACTIONS SPEAK LOUDER THAN WORDS. HOW YOU SPEAK TO PEOPLE CAN AFFECT THEM AS WELL AND SO CAN YOUR SILENCE. PEOPLE THAT ARE HURTING HURT OTHER PEOPLE. THEY ARE THE ONES THAT ARE REALLY HURTING.

"Let your life have purpose on purpose, let your life speak loud with love, let it be a message for all to hear and see the way God wants you to be."

"WITHOUT GOD THERE WOULD BE NOTHING. THANK YOU GOD FOR YOUR WORD! PRAISE GOD! GIVE GLORY TO GOD! HE IS OUR MAGNIFICENT FATHER!!

"WHEN SOMEONE OPENS THEIR HEART TO YOU FOR HELP YOU CAN GUIDE THEM AND LEAD THEM IN THE RIGHT DIRECTION. REMEMBER IT IS YOU THEY REACHED OUT TOO, STICK WITH THEM, YOU ARE THEIR GREATEST IMPACT."

YOUR JEALOUSY, INTIMIDATION, INSECURITIES AND ACTIONS ARE REALLY STARTING TO SHOW. THEY AREN'T MAKING YOU GLOW THEY ARE MAKING YOUR TRUE COLORS REALLY SHOW. IT IS SAD TO KNOW THIS IS WHAT YOU REALLY KNOW. I'LL PRAY FOR YOU SO YOU CAN LET IT ALL GO.

THE DRAGON OF THE DARKNESS ALL SOME CAN SEE IS COMPLETE DARKNESS WITH NO WAY OF ESCAPE. THEY HEAR NOTHING, SEE NOTHING THEY FEEL COMPLETE EMPTINESS, PAIN, HELPLESSNESS, HOPELESSNESS, DESPAIR AND FEAR. THEY FEEL ASHAMED, UNWANTED, UNLOVED, ETC, WITH NO WAY OUT. THE DRAGON WITHIN IS ROARING TO GET OUT!

"HOPE OVERCOMES PROLONGED EMPTINESS" Suzanne Pavlick

"I'M FAR FROM PERFECT. I COULD HAVE A FLATTER STOMACH, LONG BEAUTIFUL HAIR, A PRETTY FACE, ETC. AT LEAST I DON'T HAVE AN UGLY HEART." SPAVLICK

"Your heart shows the person you are. Fill your heart with love, kindness and compassion Your Words & Actions are Powerful! Speak and Act with Love" S Pavlick

"I KNOW WHAT I KNOW WHEN I NEED TO KNOW WHAT I KNOW WHEN I NEED TO KNOW IT, YA KNOW" SPAVLICK

"DON'T EVER WALK IN ANYONE'S SHADOW, ONLY WALK IN THE SHADOW OF THE LORD, THE ONE AND ONLY TRUE LIGHT OF THE WORLD." SPAVLICK

"Never let what people say about you or the opinions they have about you shatter you. You have a God who loves & values you Implicitly!" SP

"WE ALL WANT TOO MAKE A PLACE IN THE WORLD AND WE ALL CAN WITH LOVE." Suzanne Pavlick

"LOVE EVERYONE UNCONDITIONALLY NO MATTER WHAT, THE SAME WAY THE LORD LOVES YOU." SPAVLICK

Sometimes your response is all someone needs. Your response can be just enough to pull someone up who's feeling so low. Suzanne Pavlick

HOPE OVERCOMES EVERYTHING EVEN WHEN YOU'RE IN YOUR DARKEST MOMENTS AND THINK THERE IS NOTHING LEFT THERE IS ALWAYS HOPE NEVER EVER GIVE UP!" SUZANNE PAVLICK

RESENTMENT= POISON, IT ROBS YOU FROM SERENITY, PEACE, JOY, HAPPINESS, LOVE....IT CREATES ANGER, HATE...RESENTMENTS ARE NOT CAUSED BY OTHERS. RESENTMENT IS AN EMOTIONAL RESPONSE WITHIN YOURSELF....YOU ARE THE ONE WHO IS SUFFERING...DON'T LET OTHERS CONTROL HOW YOU FEEL... YOU CONTROL YOU!! LET GO AND LET GOD HANDLE IT, FORGIVENESS IS SUCH A BEAUTIFUL, PEACEFUL FEELING ON THE INSIDE. SUZANNE PAVLICK

WHAT ARE YOU THANKFUL FOR? I HAVE A LOT TO BE THANKFUL FOR FIRST I'M SO THANKFUL & GRATEFUL TO HAVE THE MOST AMAZING, BEAUTIFUL, FORGIVING, WONDERFUL, MAJESTIC, COMPASSIONATE, KIND, GIVING, CARING, TRUSTING & LOVING MAGNIFICENT GOD WHO FILLS MY LIFE WITH PURPOSE, HAPPINESS, JOY, PEACE & AN EVERLASTING LOVE.I THANK GOD FOR HOPE AND FAITH. I THANK GOD FOR MAKING ME STRONGER, FOR GIVING ME COURAGE & STRENGTH WHEN I NEED IT. I THANK GOD FOR ALWAYS BEING THERE FOR ME FOR WALKING BESIDES ME THROUGH THE TRIALS & TRIBULATIONS OF LIFE.I COULDN'T DO IT WITHOUT HIM. I THANK GOD FOR ALL HIS GUIDANCE & DIRECTION WITH MY LIFE AND LIFE DECISIONS. I THANK GOD FOR MY HEALTH. I AM SO THANKFUL THAT I HAVE EYES TOO SEE, EARS TO HEAR, LEGS TO WALK, ARMS TO HUG WITH, LIPS TO SMILE, A VOICE TO SPEAK, FOOD TO EAT, HEAT TO BE WARM, CLOTHES TO WEAR, A ROOF OVER MY HEAD. I THANK GOD FOR WAKING ME UP DAILY. THANK YOU GOD FOR MY BEAUTIFUL FAMILY, FRIENDS. I THANK GOD FOR ALWAYS BEING THERE AND LISTENING TO ALL MY PRAYERS. I THANK GOD FOR ALL THE BLESSINGS IN MY LIFE. THANK YOU GOD FOR ACCEPTING ME AND LOVING ME, THANK YOU, WITHOUT YOU THERE WOULD BE NO ME. WITHOUT GOD THERE WOULD BE NOTHING. THANK YOU GOD FOR YOUR WORD! PRAISE GOD!!!! GIVE GLORY TO GOD!!!!! HE IS OUR MAGNIFICENT FATHER!!!!

"TODAY WILL NEVER COME AGAIN AND TOMORROW IS PROMISED TO NOONE. BE A BLESSING TO THOSE ALL AROUND. LET YOUR WORDS TURN SOMEONE'S FROWN UPSIDE DOWN. LET YOUR WORDS LIFT UP, NOT PULL DOWN. YOU CAN SPIN SOMEONE'S LIFE AROUND. OPEN YOUR HEART, BE THE LIGHT FOR ALL TO SEE! BE A BLESSING FOR THE WORLD TOO SEE!"

WHAT'S MORE IMPORTANT? WHERE IS YOUR FOCUS?

I JUST ATTENDED A SERVICE AND AT THE SERVICE A FEW PEOPLE WERE TEXTING AND TWEETING DURING CHURCH SERVICE. I WAS SHOCKED. I THOUGHT WHEN YOU WENT TO CHURCH IT WAS TO FOCUS ON JESUS NOT YOUR CELL PHONE. I KNOW WHEN I'M PRAYING THAT HE ISN'T TEXTING OR TWEETING WHEN HE'S LISTENING TO ME OR ANSWERING MY PRAYERS. WHEN I GO TO CHURCH I GIVE GOD MY FULL UNDIVIDED ATTENTION. I'M THERE FOR HIM HE DOESN'T CARE ABOUT MY TEXT OR TWEET, HE CARES ABOUT ME BEING IN HIS HOUSE, WORSHIPPING HIM NOT MY PHONE. WHERE IS YOUR FOCUS? WHAT'S REALLY MORE IMPORTANT TO YOU? SUZANNE PAVLICK

"The only person you can control is you. When you let others control you, your life, your total world your life is no longer your own. Don't ever let anyone control you in any way shape or form. No one is worth giving up your happiness your life or your world for. Let your life be your world and your happiness be your own."
Suzanne Pavlick

"YOUR HEART SHOWS THE PERSON YOU ARE. FILL YOUR HEART WITH LOVE, KINDNESS AND COMPASSION. YOUR WORDS AND ACTIONS ARE VERY POWERFUL! THE WAY YOU ACT AND SPEAK CAN BE A HUGE IMPACT ON SOMEONE ELSE'S LIFE. OPEN YOUR HEART TO OTHERS AND SHOW THEM YOU CARE. SPEAK, ACT AND LISTEN WITH LOVE. BE THE SHINING LIGHT FOR ALL OTHERS TOO SEE." SUZANNE PAVLICK

YOU HAVE TO BELIEVE IN YOURSELF, HAVE THE COURAGE TO GO AFTER YOUR DREAMS. TAKE THAT STEP OF FAITH. HAVE FAITH IN GOD AND BELIEVE IN HIM WITH ALL YOUR HEART. HE WILL GIVE YOU THE STRENGTH, WISDOM, KNOWLEDGE & COURAGE TO FULFILL YOUR DREAMS. THE ALMIGHTY FATHER ALWAYS KEEPS HIS PROMISES.

MY FATHERS ARMS

"I feel as if I'm down deep in the depths of the ocean. I feel way, way down I keep sinking. I feel so lost without a cause. Everything is so dark, I feel like I can't breathe. I know I don't have to face it all alone. When there is no one else, I know I need to look deep within myself. Who can I turn to in times when I'm drowning in it all? As I pick up my head and look through the depths of the raging waters of the ocean I see light and can feel a beautiful presence surround me. I feel your hand touch mine I feel such a peace within me. I hear you say to me, my precious child don't cry, I'm here for you, trust me. I feel your arms as you wrap them around me. The ocean waters are also now at peace. All the pain, sorrow, sadness, darkness, depression, anxiety and fear of no tomorrow has been lifted by you. You have set me free. I can feel such an amazing release. You give me courage, strength, peace, love, joy, happiness, freedom, protection, comfort, warmth and affection. I know I never have to face anything alone. All I have to do is look to you. I surrender all to you, I trust and love you implicitly, I give my all to you. I find myself again in that familiar place in my special hiding place, IN MY FATHERS ARMS." SUZANNE PAVLICK

SILENCE IS THE LOUDEST SCREAM EVER AND CAN BE THE MOST DANGEROUS TOOL WE USE. SILENCE CAN ALSO BE A GIFT. IT HAS AN ENERGY LIKE NO OTHER SOURCE. SILENCE IS VERY POWERFUL! SILENCE SPEAKS LOUDER THAN WORDS!

By changing your attitude, opening our hearts and minds, we can change the world one person at a time. You are the only one that can change yourself. You control your behavior, attitude, openness & willingness to change. Too see things change, you need to make that change. Be that great change for all too see.

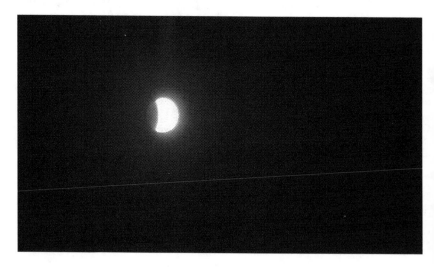

GOD MADE THE MOST REMARKABLE DIFFERENCES IN MY LIFE

I thank God for his only begotten son, Jesus Christ. God has put Love, Happiness, Peace & Joy in my heart more than I could have ever imagined. God had taught me to forgive others as he has forgiven us. God has given me the courage and strength to overcome the trials & tribulations of life. God has given me the courage to overcome fear. God says do not fear for I am with you and he will never leave you. I hold that deep in my heart. God has also said, Love everyone even your enemies and I do, even those who hate me. I pray for them also. I can't hate it's not in my heart. I love everybody no matter what. I thank God for opening up my heart more & more all the time and the most beautiful things are starting to happen not only in my heart but my mind. I can't even find the words to explain it but it's so Exquisite I can cry happy tears. God is stirring things up in me that I could've never imagined! I thank God for this beautiful life and how to look at things with an open mind and an open heart. I thank him for waking me up every day and for the opportunity to come to him anytime to pray or just talk anytime, anywhere, he is always there. I trust & believe in him with all my heart, nothing will ever change that. I thank God for my Amazing Family & Friends and the 2 most precious gifts, my children. I thank him for the people he brought into my life he has reasons why he does that and for me it's to learn from others and it has also made me stronger. Not everyone that pops into your life stays but I'm still learning. I thank him for everything in front of me, behind me, beside me & around me I can go on & on. God has shown me how to care deeply for others to reach out & help others to be kind, gentle compassionate. I thank God for his WORD. That is where I learned the True meaning of Happiness, Joy, Hope, Faith, Courage, Strength, Compassion, Peace & Love. God has made so many differences in my life & opened the door to my heart I could never thank him enough.

I love him so much! God is the Ultimate Love of My Life!!

THE MOST EXQUISITE LOVE OF ALL

"I look to you for peace, love, joy, compassion, warmth and your tender affection. My beautiful Jesus, because of you darkness is no more. You have taken me in the palm of your hands and I have risen above it all. You have shown me such a beautiful light. It has lit up my heart with an endless passion of love for you. I know the true feeling of love, joy, peace & happiness because of you. I look to you, your always there, I feel your presence all around me your warmth, love & affection with your loving arms around me. This righteous path I walk with you I know I have a beautiful future to look forward to with you. No more darkness only the beauty from above I see as your light shines over me. Jesus, you have raised me up through all the stormy seas.

I feel so free, calm & serene because your always with me."

MY EXCELLENCE, MY MAGNIFICENT MOST BEAUTIFUL LOVE OF ALL

So gentle, yet so perfect, so loving, comforting, warm, wonderful, exquisite, amazing, grateful, joyful, forgiving, kind, compassionate, giving, incomparable, magnificent and Highest of All. I look to you in times of trouble from all the pain the hurt and sorrow. When the storms are rolling in and the clouds are dark, when I am lost and broken, when I can't fight anymore even when I feel all alone and need to find an open door, there you are to give me the strength and courage to get me through. I turn to you every second of everyday. I know you will always be there with your loving arms outstretched for protection, guidance and direction. I can always feel your warmth and affection. To you I surrender all. My trust and love for you is endless for you it cannot be measured. I am nothing without you my Jesus, I Love you, Forever & Ever!

"I WILL NEVER BE ALONE AND I WILL ALWAYS BE WITH YOU

No one is promised tomorrow. We never know when our journey ends and our new journey begins. Before I go to that beautiful place of peace and rest I want you to know my love for you is forever endless. Even when I'm gone my love for you will go on and on. The MAGNIFICENT ALMIGHTY has blessed me with two of the most beautiful, precious gifts, my sunflower and super hero. I fell so deeply in love with both of you the day you were born. The day the father brought you to me. I have watched you grow into two glowing rays of sunshine and that makes my heart glow and glow. My love for you will forever flow. You are the sunshine in my life, the spring in my step, the sparkle in my eyes, the Love & joy in all my heart. We have so many beautiful memories together and you will always have them in your hearts forever. When you think of me look inside your heart that's where I'll forever be. Nothing will ever take you away from me. There have been trials in your life and I have watched you both triumph over them. They have made you stronger and braver. You both came out above. I am so proud to call you my son and daughter. You have brought me so much joy and laughter and in my heart it will be forever. You will have each other, remember what I taught you from the time you were little. Always Love one another, take care of each other, be kind, forgiving, gentle and respectful toward each other and all others. Keep your hearts and minds open, pray to God always trust and believe him with all your heart. On your life's journey follow your dreams and never let anything stop you. Believe in yourself and always remember God is always with you he's been with you from the start. He has given you the desires in your heart. God will do things that you never imagined. When it's time for me to go don't be afraid I won't be alone I'll be beside the father at his throne. Don't cry for me I want you to be happy. Wipe those tears from your face I am in a much better place.

I want you to carry on to be brave and strong. Always remember the times we shared, the laughter, Love, and the joy forever after. You have special places where you like to go and take me with you, spread my ashes for when you return I'll always be there you'll never be alone. As you look up in the sky know that I'll be looking back at you. I'll see that twinkle in your eye and feel that ray of Love from your heart. I will always Love you as I have from the start. Don't cry for me, Don't be afraid I'll never be alone I'll be in the Father's Embrace up above in a beautiful place."

By: Suzanne Pavlick Dedicated to my children Marylou & John Pavlick

THE BEAUTY WITHIN

"My Almighty Father as I walk through life's journey I see so many things. I have known all along you've been showing me things to keep me from harm. Your always there to protect me from the enemy. You have also shown me true beauty. I see the windows you have shown to me one is dark and one is beautiful. The dark window is full of hurt, pain, anger, anxiety, fear, depression, hate, control of others, judgment of others, jealousy, insecurities, violence, terror, hurtful words and hate of one another. I've seen the walls come tumbling down on others. I know this is not what you want for me it is darkness. Anyone can rise above it with you THE LIGHT OF THE WORLD. The window of beauty you have made me see. The window of HOPE, COURAGE, STRENGTH, COMPASSION, HAPPINESS, JOY, PEACE, LOVE and your PROMISES THAT I KNOW YOU ALWAYS KEEP. I know this is the window for me it is where you want me to be. Thank you my Almighty for all the beauty you have put in me. You are my End and my beginning. I look to you always and forever. You are the Light in my Life and the Beauty in my heart."

ONE OF MY DAILY PRAYERS: " I pray for World Peace for people all over the world to come together to love one another to help each other. I pray for all violence, terrorism, any unlawful acts, all the bad, the hate, Etc.to stop. Praying for the poor, needy, homeless. Praying for all who are sick, that they are healed and those who are passing are comforted. I pray for everyone to have food, shelter, clean water, for all to be happy, healthy, joyful, cheerful, prosperous, kind, compassionate & loving." **IN JESUS NAME.**

THE LIGHT OF THE WORLD THE LOVE OF MY LIFE

Father, here I am again at this familiar place down on my knees with my hands raised up to you. As I begin to pray I feel the touch of your hand on mine. I start to tremble, then cry. I can feel my body go limp as I fall into your gentle, warm, loving arms. I'm in my safe hiding place with the Love of my Life. You are the most gentle, affectionate, compassionate one! You are the blanket of security that surrounds me my protector. You are my shield, you deliver me from evil. You are my guidance, direction, my every step. You are so faithful your compassion's are new every day. You are my comforter when I'm in pain, when I'm sad, depressed, hurt, scared and worried. When I am lost or lonely you are my truest friend. You are my provider for everything. When I surrender all to you, you lift all my burdens and heaviness in my heart. You are my Ultimate Stronghold you give me courage, strength, and wisdom for everything no matter what the trial or trouble is you carry me through. You are the Great Redeemer, the restorer of all. All of my hope I put in you, I believe and trust in you with all my heart. You have given me all the peace, love and joy in my heart.

YOU ARE THE PRINCE OF PEACE, THE LIGHT OF THE WORLD, THE LOVE OF MY LIFE!

TALKING TO JESUS

"Here I am on my knees talking to Jesus as I can feel him around me. It's so quiet and calm and my heart is filled with such a beautiful peace. I came to thank you for your blessings and answered prayers not only for myself but all the world I pray for. Jesus, you always come through. You are beautifully true through and through. As I go through life's journey with you I see life in a beautiful way. I need you in every second of every day. There is no other way than to be with you Jesus the whole way. I LOVE YOU IMPLICITLY Jesus you are the music of my soul and the most beautiful love of my life."

MY PRAYER FOR EVERYONE IN THE WORLD

I PRAY THIS EVERYDAY

MY MAGNIFICENT FATHER I COME TO YOU IN PRAYER

"I pray for World Peace for people all over the world to come together to love one another to help each other. Praying for World Hunger, Poverty, Homelessness to end. Praying for all in the world to have clean water, food, shelter, medicine and all basic needs. Father I pray for all who suffer from any kind of mental illness, from suicidal thoughts & tendencies. I pray you heal and comfort the hearts of all who have gone through the loss of a child or loved one due to suicide, cancer, aids, disease, sickness, illness of any kind. I pray for all who suffer from Aids, Cancer, All diseases, sickness, illness that they are restored to good health. I pray for all those who suffer from depression, despair, anxiety, worry, fear, those struggling with any kind of problems that you heal their hearts and minds and give them the comfort they need. I pray for people not to judge one another instead love one another. I pray for all Stigma to be gone as it creates so much hate. I pray for all the violence, terrorism, fighting, wars, racism, all bad of any kind to end. For all the hate, anger, & rage to stop. I pray all can open their hearts and love one another the world would be so much more beautiful. I pray everyone would just be nice to one another, be kind, to build each other up, to encourage one another, support one another, be kind to each other, to use their words to lift each other up not tear each other down, to reach out and help one another. I pray for everyone to believe in you and trust in you with all their hearts and to realize you are THE WAY, THE TRUTH, THE LIGHT.I PRAY FOR ALL TO FIND YOU, WORSHIP YOU, PRAISE YOU, GLORIFY YOUR NAME AND FOR ALL TO LOVE YOU THE WAY YOU LOVE US ALL."

IN JESUS NAME, AMEN

I don't need material things or all kinds of money to make me happy. I don't have to pretend to be someone I'm not. I don't need a fancy car or house to make me happy. For some people the more they have the more they want. They become greedy, insecure, jealous and hateful. I wish a lot of people would realize that happiness comes from within. Having God first and foremost is the ultimate happiness. Having family, friends, and positive relationships are priceless. The love of family and friends can't be bought! Some people don't realize what they have right in front of them and how truly blessed they really are. I thank god every day for the blessings in my life. My personal relationship with god, family, friends, positive relationships, and the two most precious gifts he has given me my beautiful loving daughter and wonderful son. I'm happy and truly blessed. God is such a Magnificent God!

What a glorious and most beautiful honor it is to have the opportunity to love the most magnificent God to know the most high and to have him in my heart, mind, body, soul and strength!! I Love the Lord more than words can ever express. I cherish every moment I spend with him. They are the most precious, priceless moments ever. My Ultimate Super Hero of all. I feel so safe & secure with him he is my secret hiding place, my refuge, my strength, my comforter. His Love is immeasurable, deeper than the deepest blue seas. Nothing is Impossible for God. He is the Great Magnificent, Majestic King Forever & Ever!!!!

Printed in the United States
By Bookmasters